Progressive FINGERPICKING GUITAR LICKS

by Brett Duncan

The exercises in this book have been recorded onto a CD

Email: info@learntoplaymusic.com or visit our website on: www.learntoplaymusic.com

CD TRACK LISTING

#	Track	#	Track
1	Tuning	17	Ex 31-32
2	Ex 1-4	18	Ex 33-34
3	Ex 5-8	19	Ex 35-36
4	Ex 9-12	20	Ex 37-38
5	Ex 13-16	21	Ex 39-40
6	Ex 17-20	22	The Entertainer
7	Ex 21-22	23	Geoffrey's Rag
8	Ex 23-24	24	Chordial Chaos
9	Betty's Blues	25	Pineapple Rag
10	The Old Man	26	Ex 41
11	C for Yourself	27	Ex 42
12	Constant Velocity	28	Ex 43
13	Ex 25	29	Ex 44
14	Ex 26	30	Ex 45
15	Ex 27-28	31	Ex 46
16	Ex 29-30		

Acknowledgements
Cover Photograph: Phil Martin

Email: info@learntoplaymusic.com
www.learntoplaymusic.com

I.S.B.N. 0 947183 70 1
Order Codes:
   CD Pack   CP-18370

COPYRIGHT CONDITIONS
No part of this book can be reproduced in any form without written consent of the publisher.

© 2002 L.T.P. Publishing Pty. Ltd.

Contents

	Page
Introduction	4
Notation, Tablature Symbols, Chord Diagrams, Scales	5

		Page
Section I	**Chord Licks and Supplements**	**7**
Lesson 1	E Chord Licks	8
Lesson 2	A Chord Licks	10
Lesson 3	G Chord Licks	12
Lesson 4	C Chord Licks	14
Lesson 5	D Chord Licks	16
Lesson 6	F Chord Licks	18
Lesson 7	B Chord Licks	20
Supplement 1	Betty's Blues	22
Supplement 2	The Old Man	24
Supplement 3	C For Yourself	26
Supplement 4	Constant Velocity	28
Section II	**Monotonic Bass Solos**	**30**
Lesson 8	Monotonic Bass Solo 1	30
Lesson 9	Monotonic Bass Solo 2	32
Section III	**Extended Chord Licks and Supplements**	**34**
Lesson 10	Extended E Chord Licks	35
Lesson 11	Extended A Chord Licks	36
Lesson 12	Extended G Chord Licks	37
Lesson 13	Extended C Chord Licks	38
Lesson 14	Extended D Chord Licks	39
Lesson 15	Extended F Chord Licks	40
Lesson 16	Extended B Chord Licks	41
Supplement 5	The Entertainer	42
Supplement 6	Geoffrey's Rag	46
Supplement 7	Chordial Chaos	50
Supplement 8	Pineapple Rag	54
Section IV	**Open Tunings**	**58**
Lesson 17	Open G Tuning	59
	Jewels	60
	Gee Wizz	61
Lesson 18	Open D Tuning	62
	Siberia	63
Lesson 19	Open C Tuning	64
	Backyard Boogie	65
Lesson 20	Open E Tuning	66
	The Longest Mile	67
	Country Stomp	68

Introduction

Progressive Fingerpicking Guitar Licks has been designed to expand your knowledge and technique needed to play contemporary styles of Fingerpicking guitar.

It will be necessary to have a basic knowledge of fingerpicking in order to begin the first section (See Progressive Fingerpicking Guitar by Gary Turner and Brenton White.) The licks outlined in the book are based upon popular chord shapes used by fingerpicking guitarists and have been carefully graded into order of difficulty.

SECTION ONE uses some common licks with the open position chords. These licks will give the player a wider knowledge of fingerpicking basic chords and may be applied to any chord progression. The supplements with section one are examples of how you can arrange these licks into a fingerpicking guitar solo. An analysis preceeding each tune will describe how the previous licks have been used in the supplements.

SECTION TWO consists of two examples which preview the use of a monotonic bass line. This style was mostly used in the 1920's by the Mississippi Blues Men.

SECTION THREE is made up of popular riffs used on other parts of the fretboard. These riffs will add variety to any finger picker's repertoire. Supplements are added at the end of this section based upon the previous extended chord licks.

SECTION FOUR introduces open tunings which have been widely used in contemporary guitar for many years.

Every guitar player will find something useful in this manual whether they wish to apply the riffs and supplements to rock, blues, country, folk or any of the many other styles of music where the guitar is used.

Good luck,

BRETT DUNCAN

Progressive Fingerpicking Guitar Solos

Progressive Fingerpicking Guitar Solos by Brett Duncan is a collection of great sounding fingerpicking solos covering all styles of contemporary fingerpicking guitar such as Blues, Ragtime, Country, Boogie and Classical. The solos in the book can be used to supplement the material found in Progressive Fingerpicking Licks. Also included is an open tuning fingerpicking solo and an acoustic slide solo. Several appendices covering music theory for guitar and a chord chart appears at the end of the book.

Notation

This book uses standard music notation and tablature notation. If you cannot read music notes use the tab written below the music. Music readers will need to look at the tab to see what technique is being used to play certain notes (e.g. hammer, slide etc.)

Tablature

Tablature is a method of indicating the position of notes on the fretboard. There are six "tab" lines each representing one of the six strings on the guitar:

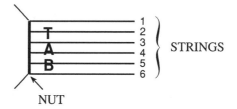

When a number is placed on one of the lines, it indicates the fret location of a note. e.g.

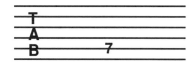

This indicates the 7th fret of the 5th string (an E note).

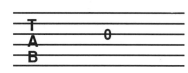

This indicates the third string open (a G note).

Tablature Symbols

The Hammer
A curved line and the letter H indicates a hammer. The first note is played but the second note is produced by hammering on the left hand finger which plays the second note.

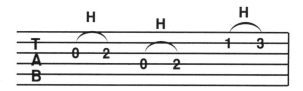

The Pull-Off
A curved line and the letter P indicates a pull-off. The first note is played but the second note is produced by pulling off the finger which is playing the first note.

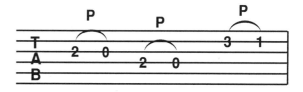

The Slide
The letter S and a straight line represents a slide. If the line comes from below the number, slide from a lower fret but if the line is above the number, slide from a higher fret. The third example on the right shows the desired fret to slide from.

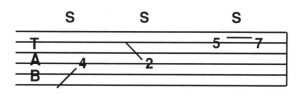

The Bend
The letter B and a curved line represents a bend. The note is played by the left hand finger which bends the string (from the note indicated in the tab).

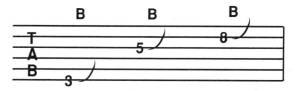

Chord Diagrams

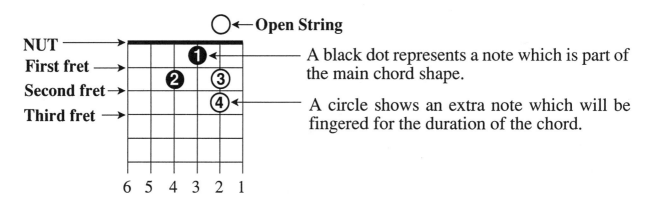

Technique Symbols

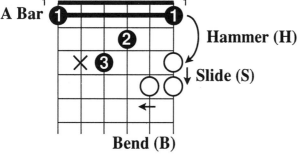

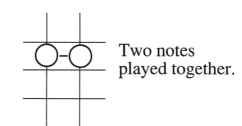

Two notes played together.

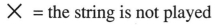

✗ = the string is not played

Scales

The two types of scales you will use in this book are the Major scale and the Blues scale.

The Major scale is a series of eight notes in alphabetical order that has the familiar sound Do Re Mi Fa So La Ti Do.

e.g. C Major scale

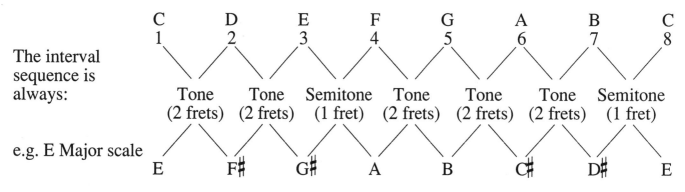

The Blues scale consists of the 1 – ♭3 – 4 – ♭5 – 5 – ♭7
notes of the Major scale. (For more information on scales see Progressive Lead Guitar).

e.g. C Blues scale   C   E♭   F   G♭   G   B♭

e.g. E Blues scale   E   G   A   B♭   B   D

SECTION I

Chord Licks and Supplements

Lesson 1
E Chord Licks

The first thing you must learn when fingerpicking a chord is the bass line. The standard bass line for an E chord alternates between the open E string (sixth string) and the E note on the second fret of the fourth string.

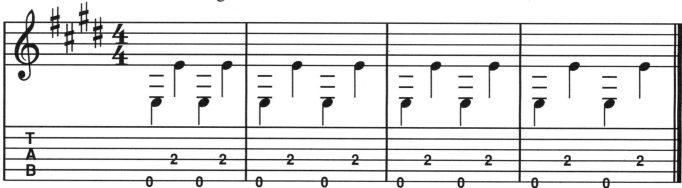

While the right hand thumb is playing the standard bass line, the right hand fingers are playing a melody on the first three strings. The notes which are played are taken from the E Major scale and the E Blues scale.

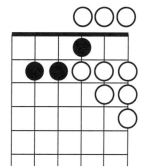

Optional E Major with Hammer

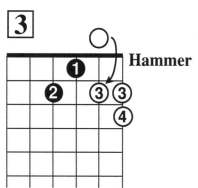

Hammer Example One is played by using an optional E Major fingering. A hammer is used on the third string.

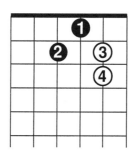

Example Two uses two extra notes from the E Sixth and the E Seventh chords.

Example Three uses the second and third frets of the first string to expand the melody as well as another hammer on the second string.

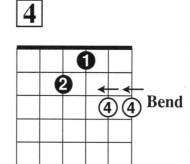

Example Four shows how to bend the note on the third fret of the first and second string as an extra effect.

Lesson 2
A Chord Licks

The standard alternating bass line for an A chord uses the open fifth string and the second fret on the fourth string (an E note).

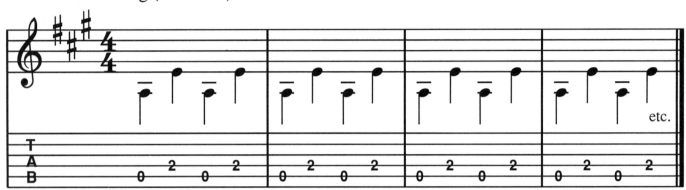

As with Lesson One use the A Major and A Blues scales as melody notes, along with the standard A chord alternating bass line.

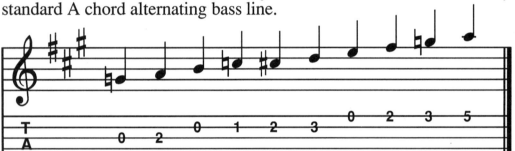

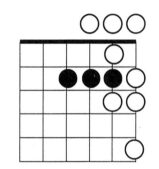

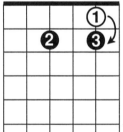

Hammer Example Five uses an A Seventh chord as a basis. The third finger plays a hammer on the second string.

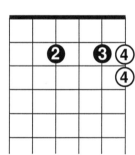

Example Six uses some extra notes from the A Sixth and A Seventh chords.

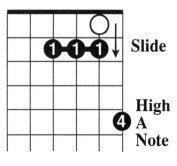

Example Seven is played with a half bar on the second fret and the fourth finger holding the top A note on the fifth fret. A slide is also used on the second string. When playing the slide, slide the half bar from the first fret.

Slide

High A Note

Example Eight shows how you can harmonize (i.e. play two or more notes together) the high A note and the seventh note with the C♯ on the second string.

Lesson 3
G Chord Licks

The standard alternating bass line for a G chord is between the notes G on the third fret of the sixth string and the open fourth string (a D note).

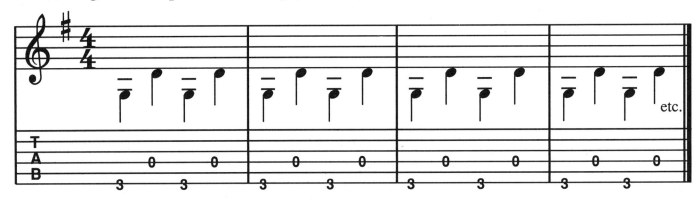

The melody notes used with the above bass line are taken from the G Major Scale and the G blues scale.

 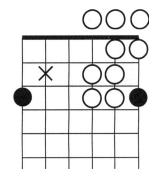

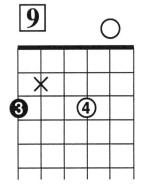

Example Nine shows a popular way of using the B♮ and B♭ in the melody. Try not to sustain these two notes together.

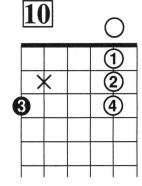

Example Ten uses the extra notes on the second string. Pay special attention to the fingering.

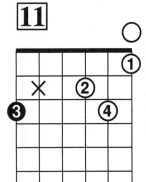

Example Eleven combines the G Sixth and the G Seventh chord. Also observe the A note which is used in the last bar.

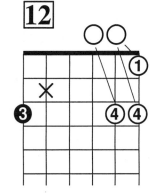

Example Twelve is similar to Example Eleven but shows how you can use a harmony on the second and third strings.

Lesson 4
C Chord Licks

The standard alternating bass line for a C chord is between the C note on the third fret of the fifth string and the E note on the second fret of the fourth string.

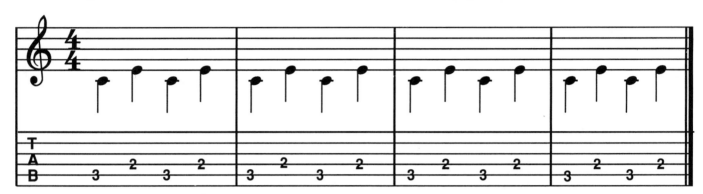

Once again use the notes from the C Major and Blues scales for the melody.

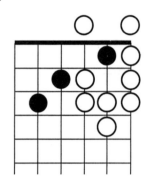

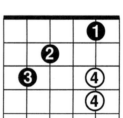

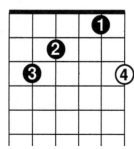

Example Thirteen uses a C Major with a C seventh chord.

Example Fourteen uses two extra notes on the second string.

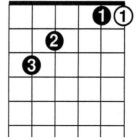

Example Fifteen adds the top G note on the first string.

Example Sixteen uses the F note on the first string as well as the other notes in the previous three exercises.

Lesson 5
D Chord Licks

When you fingerpick a D Major chord there are three standard bass lines. The key note (D) is on the open fourth string. Below are the three different bass lines used in Exercises 17 to 20.

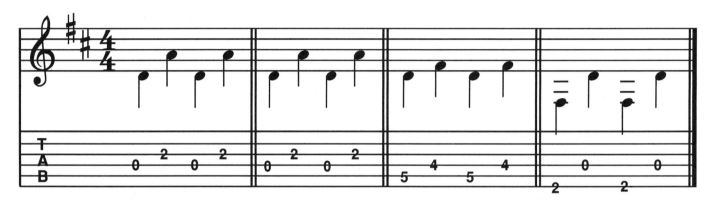

The melody notes used for the D major chord are a mixture of the D Major scale and the D Blues scale.

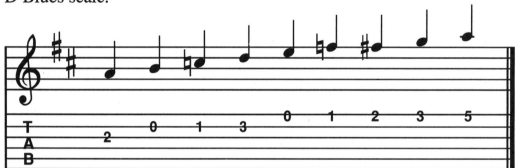
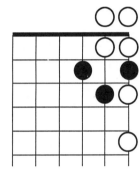

17

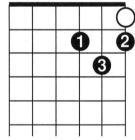

Slide

Example Seventeen uses a slide from the first fret on the first string. Slide the entire D chord for convenience.

18

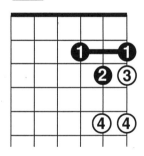

Example Eighteen is played with a bar on the second fret so you can play the top A note on the fifth fret.

19

Example Nineteen is a commonly used shape. It is a C7 chord moved up the fretboard two frets.

20

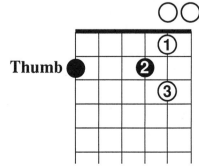

Example Twenty is another popular shape used for D Major licks. Note the use of the F# bass note played with the thumb.

Lesson 6
F Chord Licks

The F Major licks are based upon the Root Six bar chord. These licks are moveable, i.e. they can be played in any position on the fretboard. The standard bass line alternates between the octave notes of the sixth and fourth strings. A complete discussion of bar chords can be found in Progressive Rhythm Guitar.

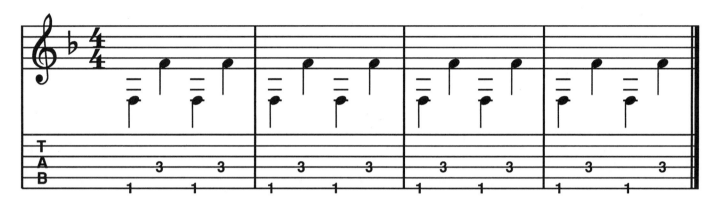

The melody notes are taken from the F Major scale and the F Blues scale.

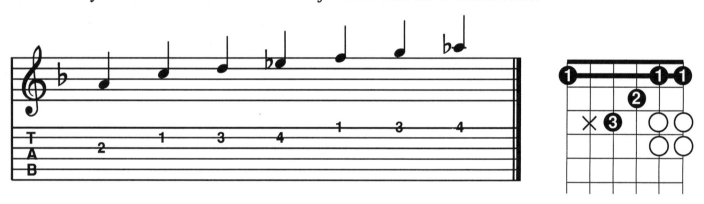

21

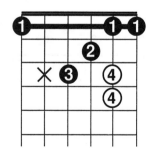

Example Twenty One uses two notes from the F Major Sixth and the F Seventh chords.

22

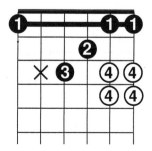

Example Twenty Two is similar to example Twenty One but uses extra notes on the first string as well as a harmony between both strings.

Lesson 7
B Chord Licks

There are two common bass lines used for the B chord licks. Example 23 is based upon the basic B Seventh chord and Example 24 is using the B Major Root Five bar chord.

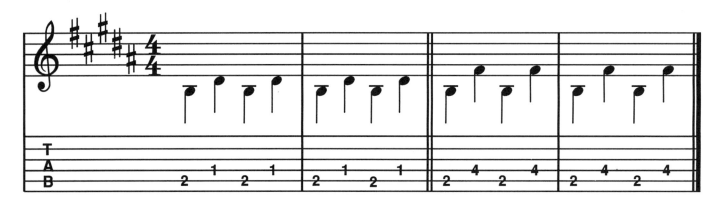

The melody notes used in both examples are notes from the B Major and B Blues scale.

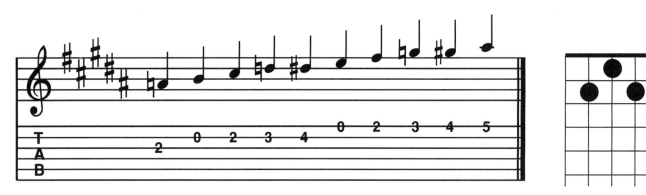

23

Example Twenty Three uses the basic B Seventh shape with extra notes from the first and second strings.

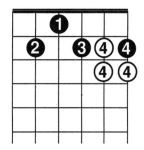

24

Example Twenty Four is based around the B Seventh bar chord. Note the hammer on the second string.

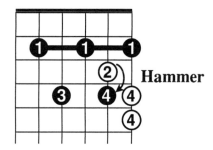

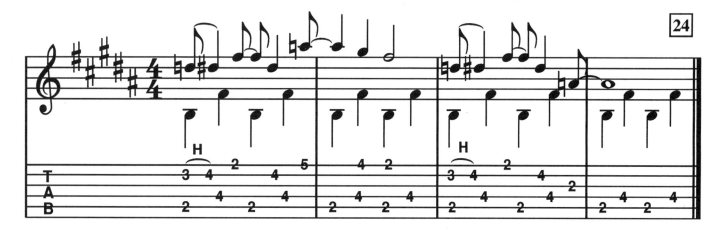

Supplement 1
Betty's Blues

The first supplement is based upon a twelve bar blues progression in the key of E Major.

12 Bar Blues in E

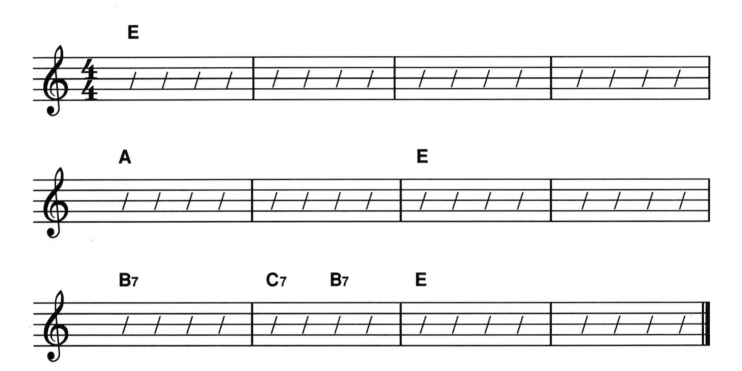

Betty's Blues – Analysis

- Bars one and two are taken directly from Lesson One, E Chord Licks, Example Two.
- Bars three and four are also from Lesson One. This time Example Four.
- Bars five and six are represented in Lesson Two, A Chord Licks, Example Six.
- Bars seven and eight are also from Lesson One, Example Four.
- Refer to Lesson Seven for bar number nine.
- In bar number ten move the basic B Seventh chord up the fret board one fret to play the C Seventh.
- The supplement finishes with the same lick as in bars three and four.

Betty's Blues

Chord shapes used in "Betty's Blues".

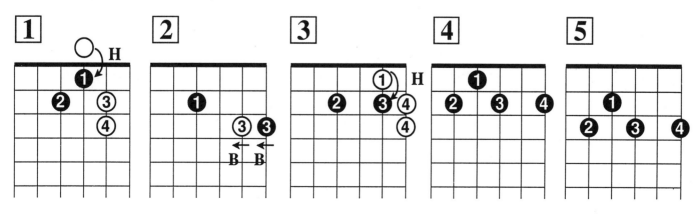

Supplement 2
The Old Man

Supplement Number Two is a twelve bar blues progression in the key of G Major.

12 Bar Blues in G

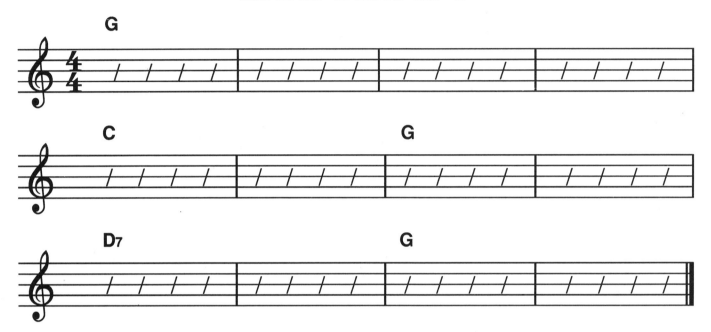

The Old Man - Analysis

- Bars one to four use some of the G chord licks played in Lesson Three.

- Bars five and six are variations on the examples we found in Lesson Four, C Chord Licks.

- Bars seven and eight are the same as bar three and four. Refer to Lesson Three, G Chord Licks for the very same lick.

- In Lesson Five, D Chord Licks, Example Nineteen you will find a similar lick to bars nine and ten.

- The final two bars introduce your first turnaround in the key of G. A turnaround is a common lick found at the end of a blues progression.

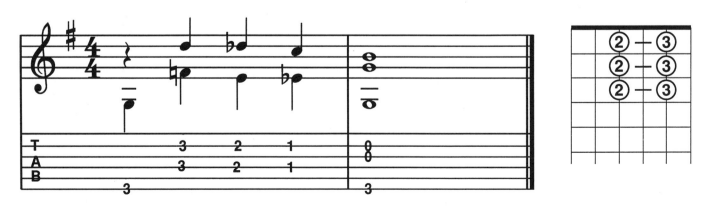

The Old Man

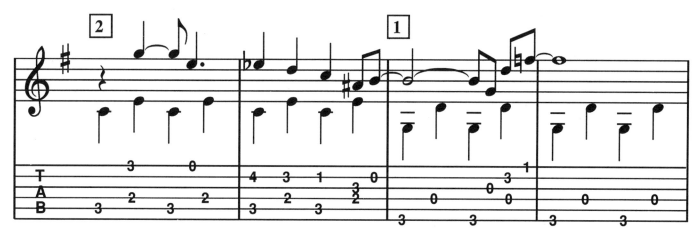
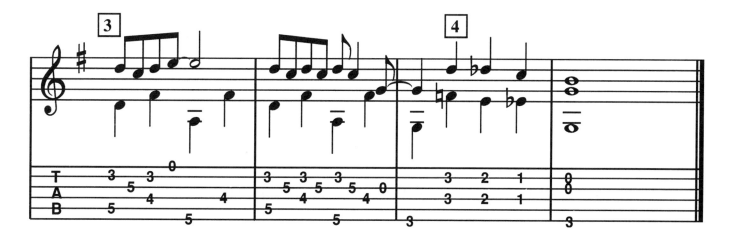

Chord shapes used in "The Old Man".

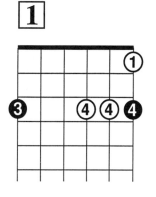
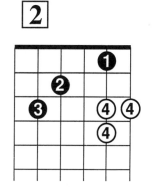
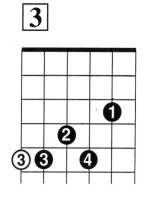
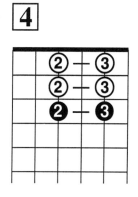

Supplement 3
C For Yourself

This supplement is a twelve bar blues progression in the key of C Major.

12 Bar Blues in C

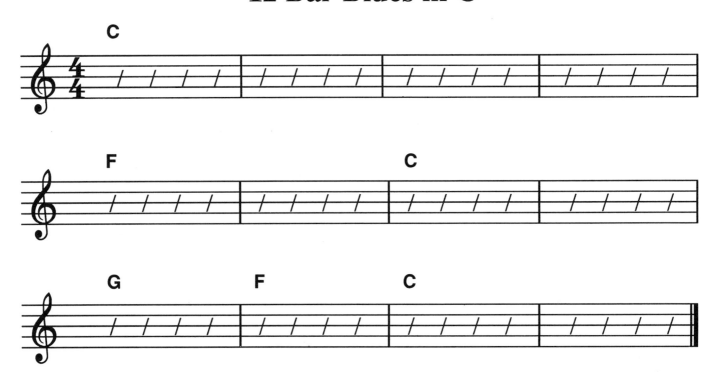

C For Yourself – Analysis

- The first four bars are based upon the licks in Lesson Four, C Chord Licks.
- Refer to Lesson Six, F Chord Licks for bars five and six.
- Bars seven and eight use a walking bass line and bar eight uses triplets. To understand triplet timing listen to the recording or see Progressive Rhythm Guitar.
- Bar nine is a G Chord Lick from Lesson Three and bar ten is a F Chord Lick from Lesson Six.
- The final two bars consist of a tag. This is a single note run from the C Blues scale. The right hand fingers should play strings 1 to 3 and the right hand thumb will play strings 4 to 6.

C For Yourself

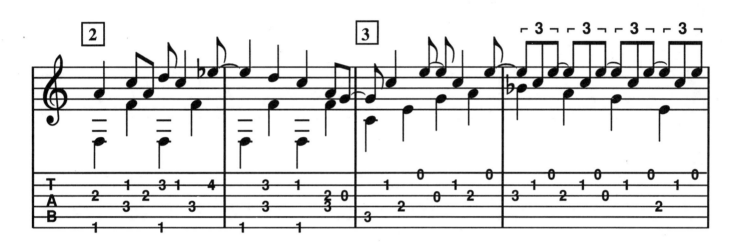

Chord shapes used in "C For Yourself".

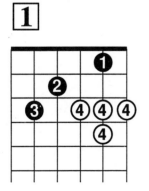
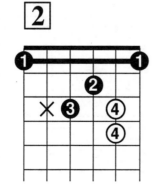
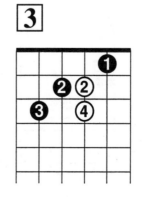
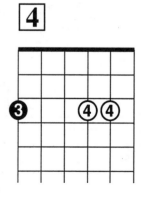

Supplement 4
Constant Velocity

Supplement four is another twelve bar blues progression. This time it is in the key of A Major.

12 Bar Blues in A

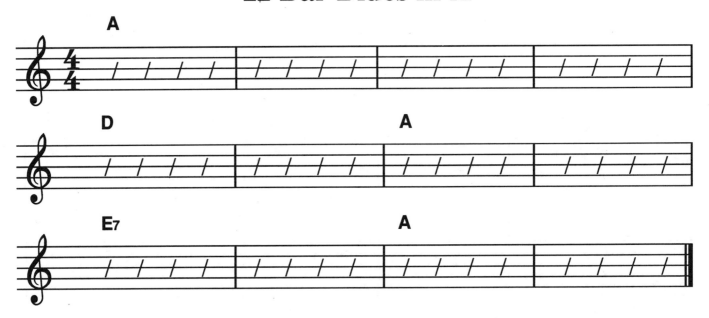

Constant Velocity – Analysis

- Bars one to four are almost directly taken from Example Seven, Lesson Two, A Chord Licks.

- Bars five and six are found in Example Twenty, Lesson Five, D Chord Licks.

- Bars seven and eight are examples of a harmonized melody line. Notice the melody descending on the first string as the harmony is ascending on the second string.

- Bars nine and ten are based upon an E Seventh chord with a walking bass and melody line to lead back to the A Major chord.

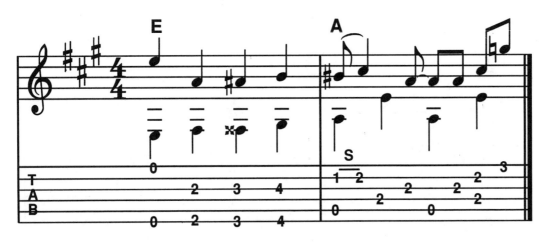

Constant Velocity

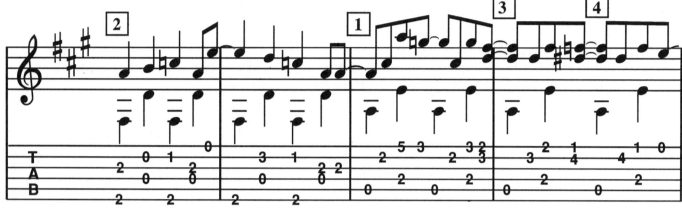
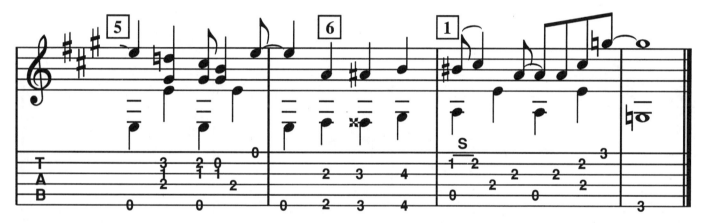

Chord shapes used in "Constant Velocity".

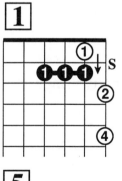
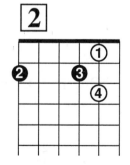
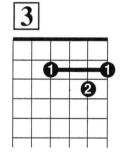
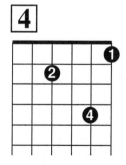
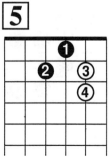
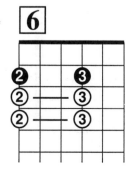

SECTION II
Monotonic Bass Solos

Lesson 8

The difference between the monotonic bass solos and the previous exercises is in the bass line. The bass line for these pieces is a droning root bass note on each beat of the bar instead of the alternating bass line we have mainly used in the other supplements.

Example 25

The first example is in the key of E Major and is based upon a twelve bar blues progression similar to Supplement Number One on page 22.

The three bass lines used are for the E Major, A Major and B Seventh chords.

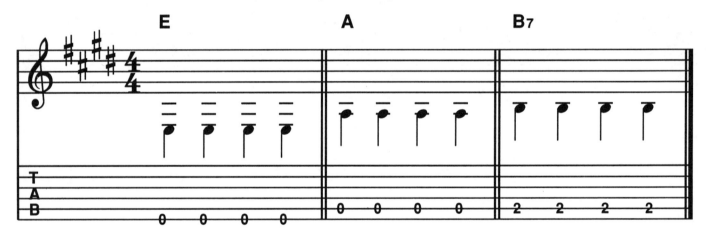

The melody in Example Twenty Five is taken from the E Blues scale. An alternative fingering (written in brackets) has been given for the open first and second strings.

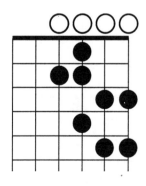

Monotonic Bass Solo 1

Lesson 9

Example 26

The next example is in the key of A and is based upon a 12 bar blues progression as found in Supplement Four on page 28.

The three bass lines used for Example Twenty Six are the Root Bass notes of the A Major, D Major and E Major chords.

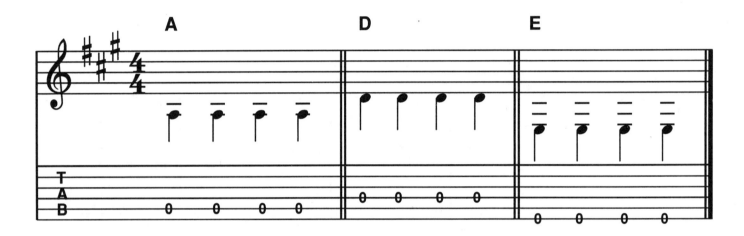

The melody this time is made up of notes from the A Blues scale.

 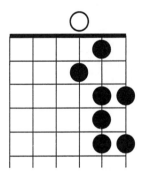

Monotonic Bass Solo 2

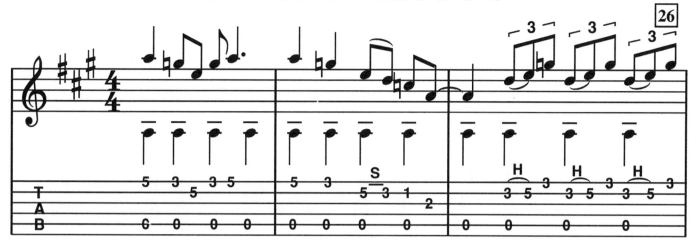
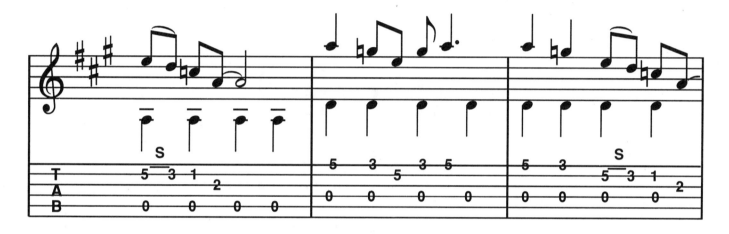
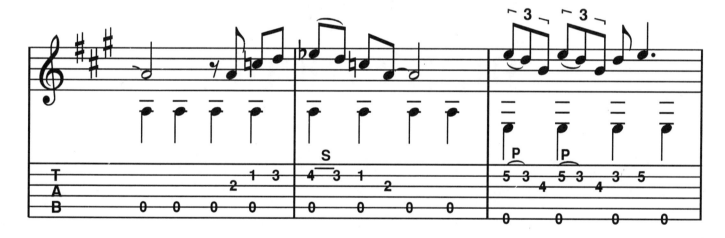
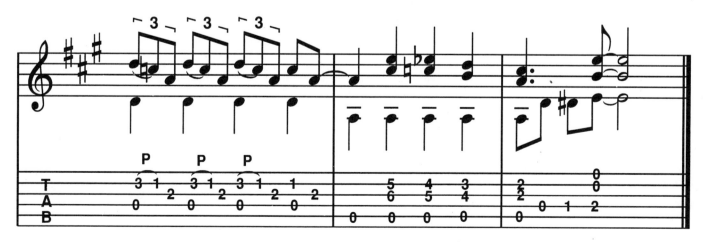

SECTION III

Extended Chord Licks and Supplements

Lesson 10

The licks in this section include many popular riffs played higher up the fretboard. Many are based on bar chord shapes. For more information on bar chords see Progressive Rhythm Guitar.

Extended E Chord Licks

27

Example Twenty Seven uses a popular E Major chord on the seventh fret. The bass note is played with the first finger and the first string note is played with the second finger. The third finger bends the second string and the fourth finger plays the extra notes on the ninth fret.

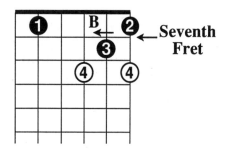

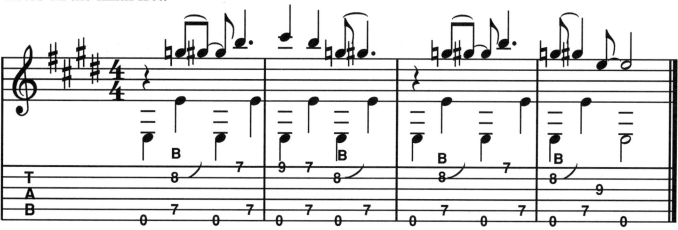

28

Example Twenty Eight is a half bar on the ninth fret with the fourth finger playing the twelfth fret on the first string. The entire shape slides from the eighth fret to obtain the slide in bars two and four.

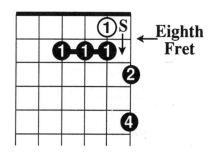

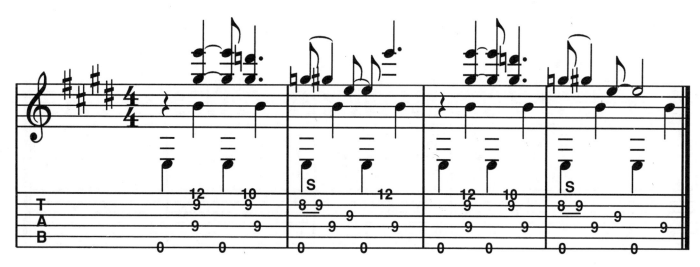

Lesson 11
Extended A Chord Licks

29

Example Twenty Nine uses an extended A chord on the fifth fret with the long A shape in the open position. You will find similar riffs in Lesson Two - A Chord Licks.

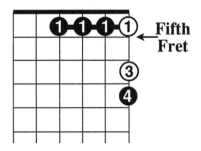

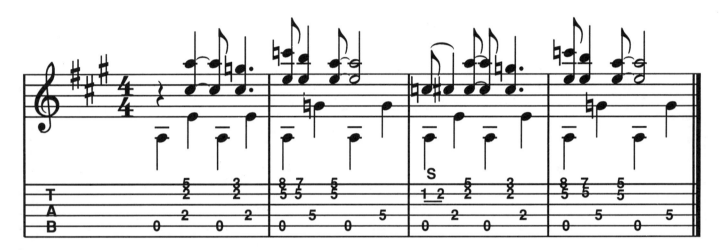

30

Example Thirty is an interesting way of using a basic A Seventh chord. The right hand thumb plays a walking bass line. Either the left hand thumb or first finger can be used to play the F# on the sixth string.

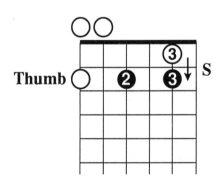

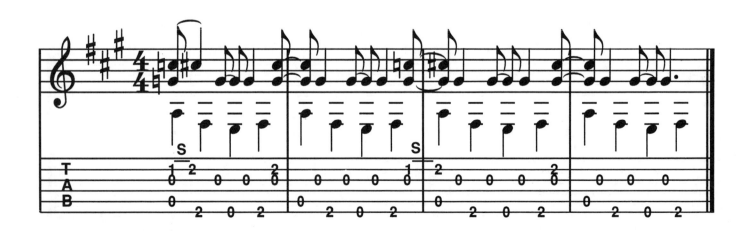

Lesson 12
Extended G Chord Licks

31

Example Thirty One uses two different extended G chord licks. The first is similar to the licks found in Lesson Six - F Chord Licks. The second extension is played on the tenth fret with the bass line played on the open third and fourth strings.

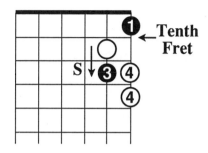

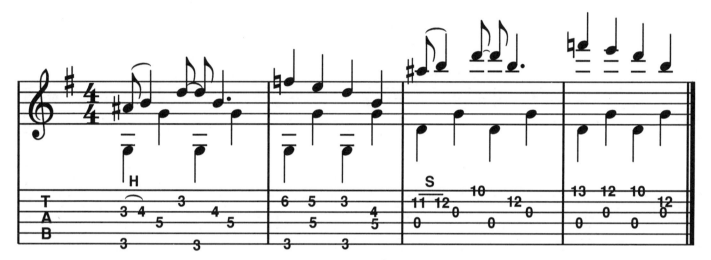

32

Example Thirty Two is based upon some of the tricks used in Lesson Three - G Chord Licks but uses a more complicated bass line. Notice the left hand fingering to play the bass notes on the fourth string.

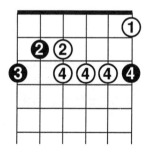

Lesson 13
Extended C Chord Licks

[33]

Example Thirty Three combines the basic C chord with a half bar on the fifth fret. The fourth finger plays the top "C" note and the second and third fingers play the extra two notes on the first string.

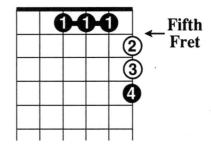

[34]

Example Thirty Four shows the C Seventh bar chord on the third fret as an extended shape with two examples of a single note run taken from the C Blues scale.

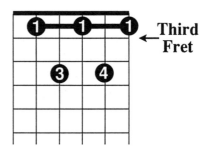

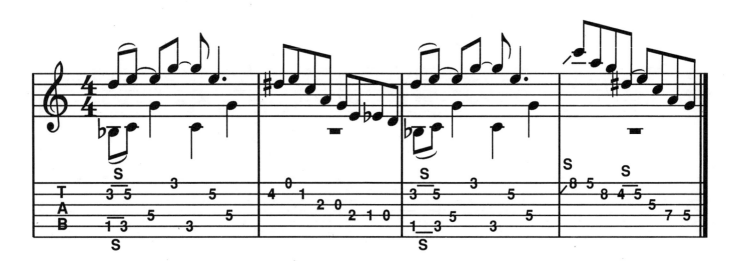

Lesson 14
Extended D Chord Licks

35

Example Thirty Five is based upon an extended D chord on the fifth fret. The fourth finger provides the hammer on the first string.

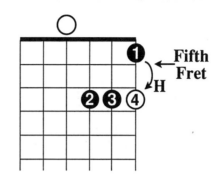

36

Example Thirty Six is a half bar on the seventh fret with the fourth finger playing the top "D" note on the tenth fret. As with Example Thirty Five the thumb alternates between the fourth and third strings.

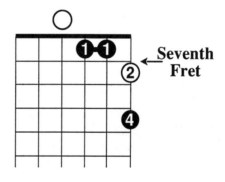

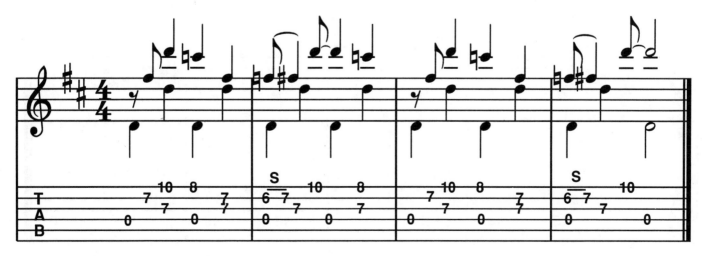

Lesson 15
Extended F Chord Licks

37

Example Thirty Seven is an F Seventh chord played on the sixth fret. The fourth finger plays the extra notes on the eighth and ninth frets and the first finger plays the top "B♭" note on the first string.

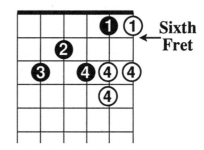

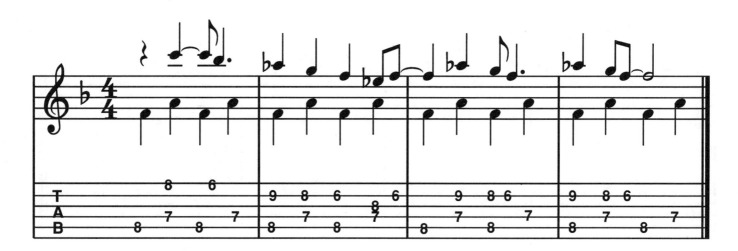

38

Example Thirty Eight uses the Root Five Seventh bar chord. The hammer is used with the second and fourth fingers. The fourth finger also plays the two extra notes on the first string.

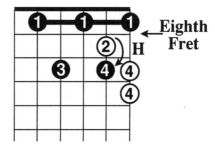

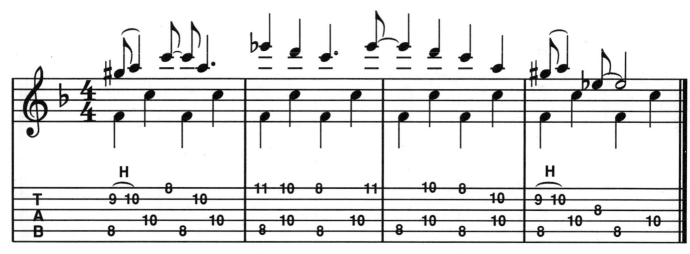

Lesson 16
Extended B Chord Licks

39

Example Thirty Nine uses a riff taken from Lesson Seven - B Chord Licks, as well as the first extension on the fourth fret. The bar slides from the second fret at the beginning of the third measure and the other fingers play a familiar descending lick on the first string.

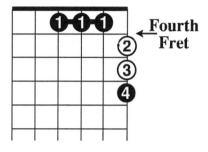

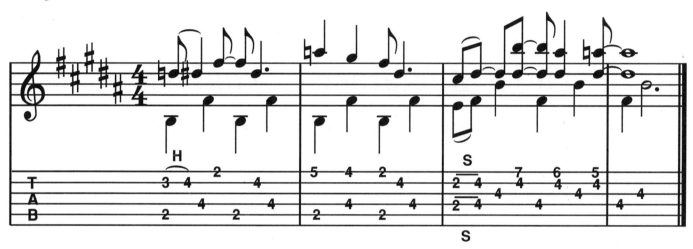

40

Example Forty utilizes the hammer to obtain a honky-tonk sound in the melody. The shape is a standard Root Six Seventh bar on the seventh fret.

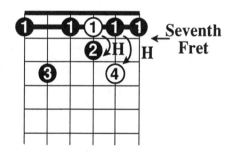

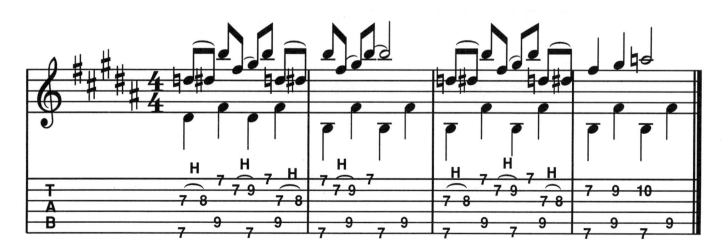

Supplement 5

The Entertainer

This arrangement is in the key of G Major and consists of the first two sections of the original song. Most of the solo can be related to some of the licks shown at the beginning of this book but a walking bass line is used more often than previous examples.

After the four bar introduction, the traditional sequence for playing a rag is to play the first section twice then the second section twice and finally section one again.

The Entertainer – Analysis

- The introduction is played with the right hand fingers controlling the first three strings and the right hand thumb playing the three lower bass strings.

- During section one most of the licks can be found in Lesson Three - G Chord Licks. Measures six and eight are where the first bass runs are used. It is important to sustain each bass note and play them a little louder.

- The final four bars of the first section have a bass line which descends almost the entire G Major scale. The bass line must once again be played a little louder.

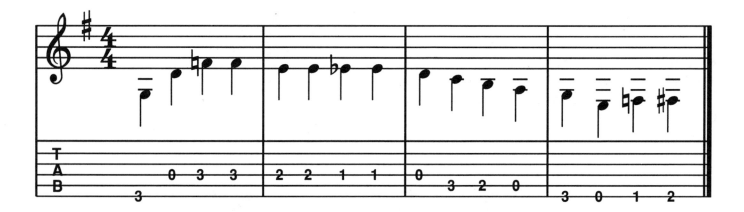

- Section two uses mainly riffs which can be found in both Lesson Three - G Chord Licks and Lesson Four - C Chord Licks.

Chord shapes used in "The Entertainer".

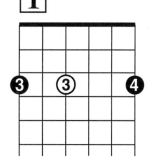 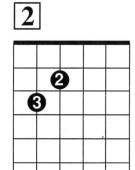 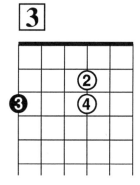 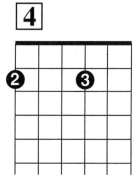

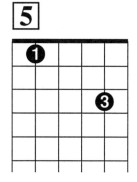 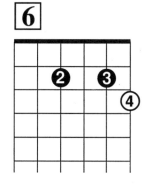 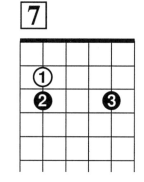 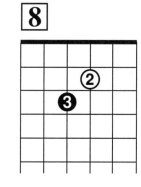

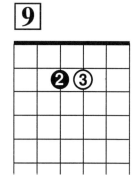 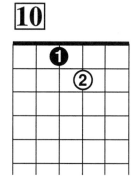 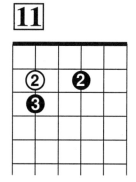 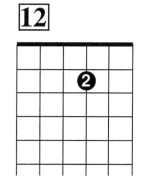

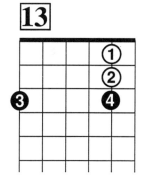 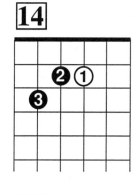 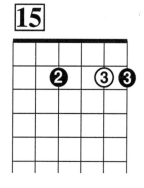 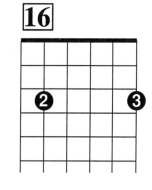

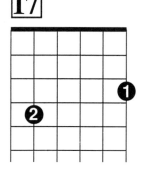 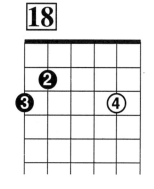 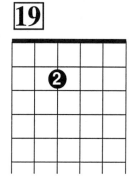

The Entertainer

Scott Joplin

Supplement 6

Geoffrey's Rag

Geoffrey's Rag is in the key of C and uses a cliche ragtime progression. The first verse uses riffs taken directly from the first section of chord licks at the beginning of the book. The second half of the solo is an example of how some of the extended chord licks can be used.

Geoffrey's Rag – Analysis

- This tune opens with a turnaround in the key of C. Begin with a bar on the third fret and guide your fourth finger down the second string.

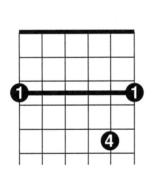 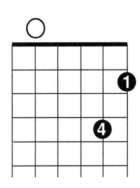 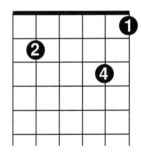

- Section one is a mixture of riffs found at the beginning of the book in Lessons Two, Three, Four and Five.

- Refer to the extended chord licks for the A Major, D Major and G Major chords found in the second section of the solo.

- The single note run in the middle of the second verse is similar to example 34 in the extended C Major licks.

- The final two measures of the second verse are an example in playing part of the melody in octaves and intervals of thirds. Use the thumb for all the lower notes.

Chord shapes used in "Geoffrey's Rag".

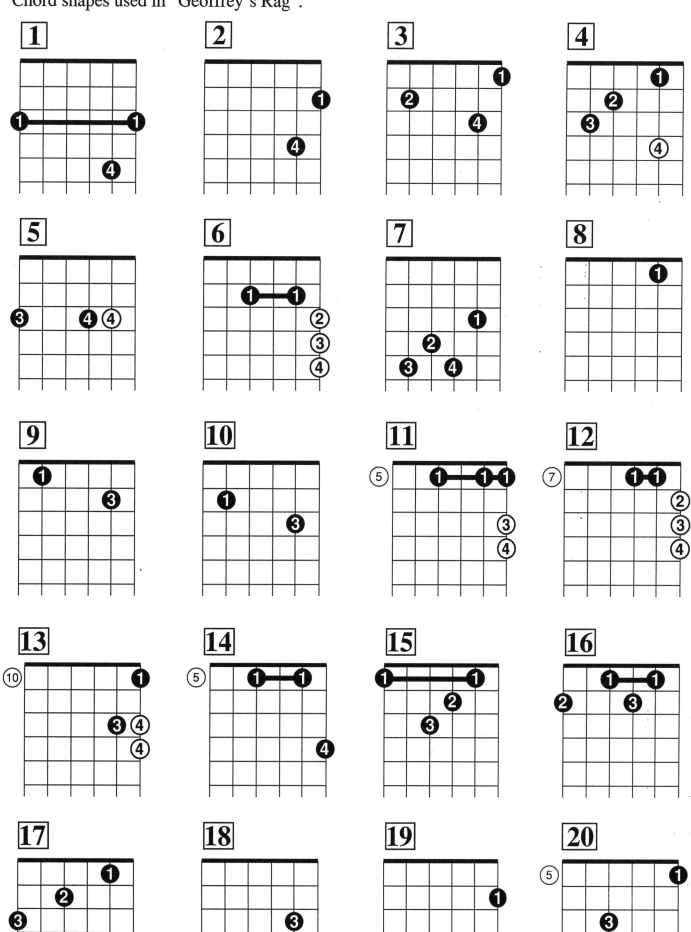

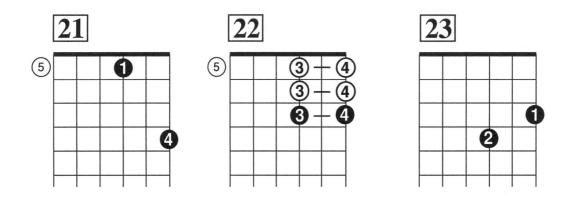

Geoffrey's Rag

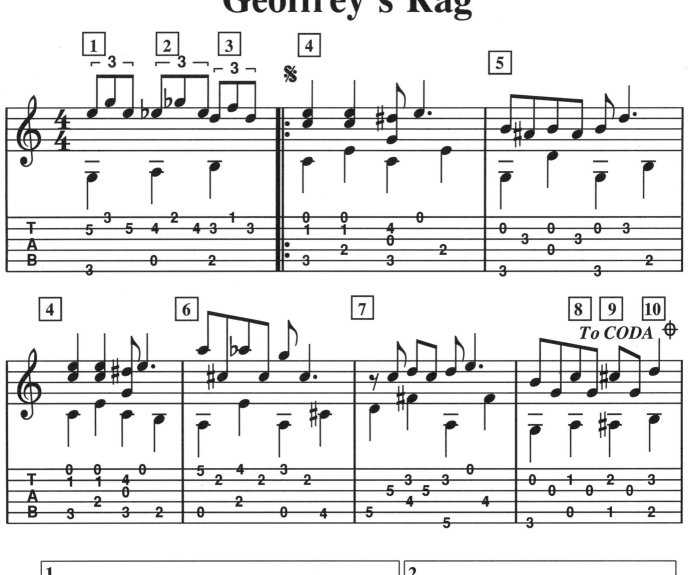
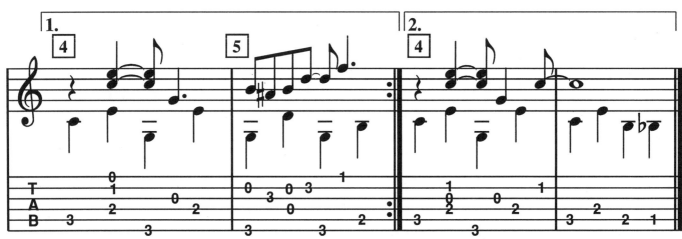

Supplement 7
Chordial Chaos

Supplement Seven is a solo in the key of E Major and has an eight bar blues progression for the first verse and a traditional sixteen bar ragtime progression for the second verse.

Eight Bar Blues Progression

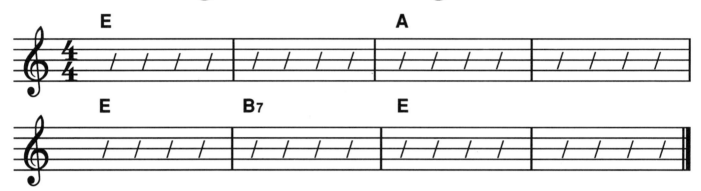

Sixteen Bar Ragtime Progression

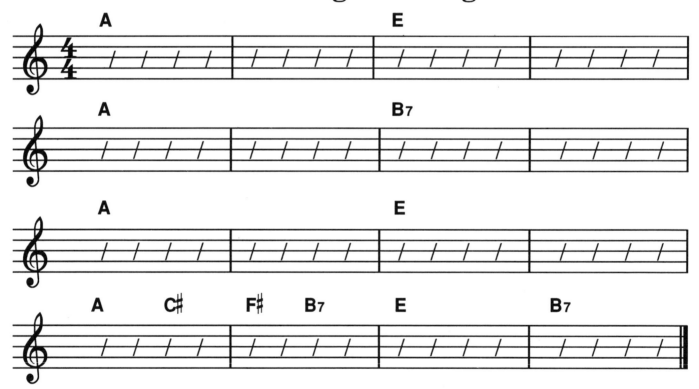

Chordial Chaos – Analysis

- The first two measures use extended E chord lick, Example Twenty Seven. Several jazz chords have been used to add a different sound than previous supplements. Be sure to play the walking bass line clearly.

- To play the single note bass lick which is dominant throughout the second verse use your right hand thumb for the sixth string and your fingers for the fifth and fourth strings.

Chord shapes used in "Chordial Chaos".

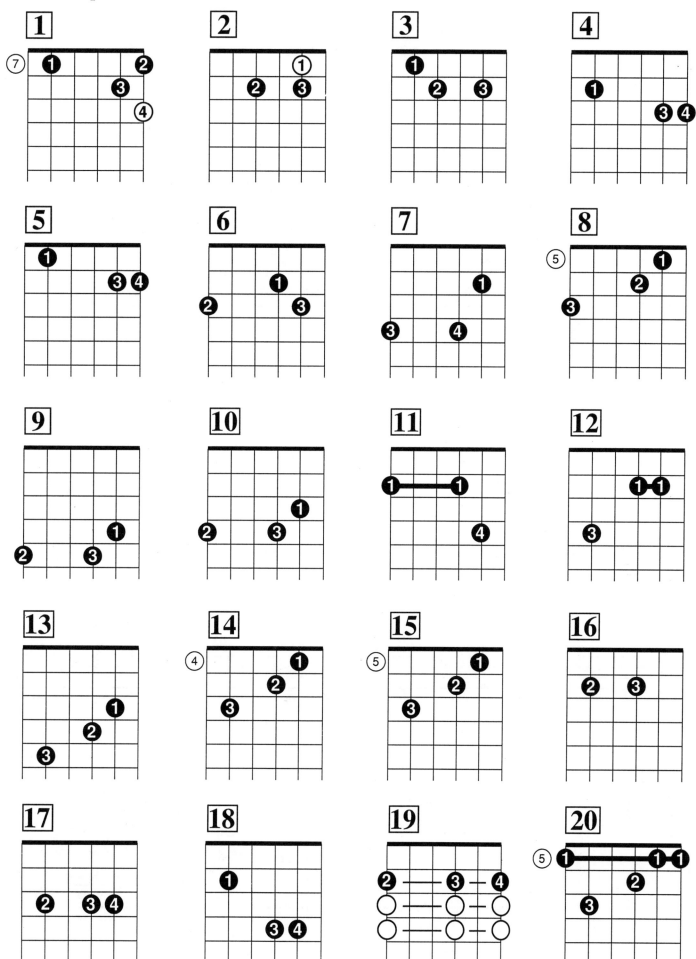

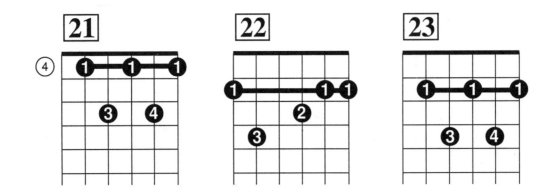

Chordial Chaos

Harm. = Harmonic. For more information on harmonics see Progressive Lead Guitar.

Supplement 8
Pineapple Rag

Pineapple Rag is another piece by Scott Joplin which uses a sixteen bar ragtime progression. It is probably the most difficult piece so far and takes a lot of control with the left hand to bring out the effect of the bass line.

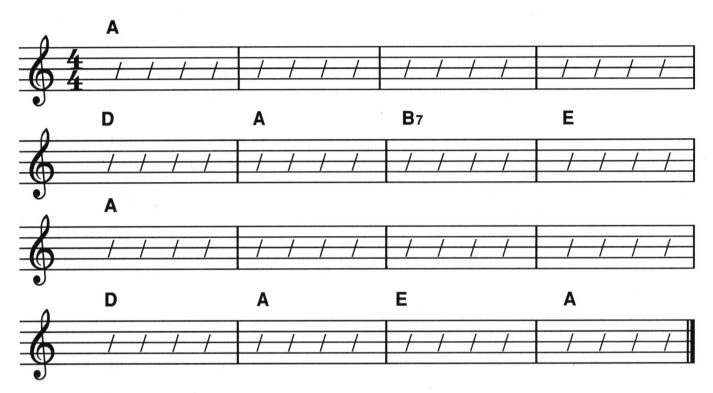

Pineapple Rag – Analysis

- The introduction is typical of a ragtime solo and quite often is played in octaves. Balance the bass and melody as even as possible.

- The first and third lines of the first verse use the long A shape as found in Lesson Two – A Chord Licks.

- Notice the backward bass line in measures five and thirteen and the descending bass line in measures six and eight. Try to sustain the notes as long as possible.

- The second verse uses a very different bass line to what has been used previously. Eighth notes are used so the right hand thumb must double its normal rhythm.

Chord shapes used in "Pineapple Rag".

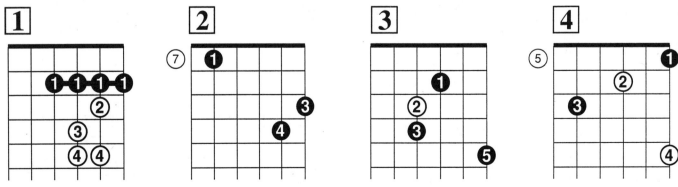

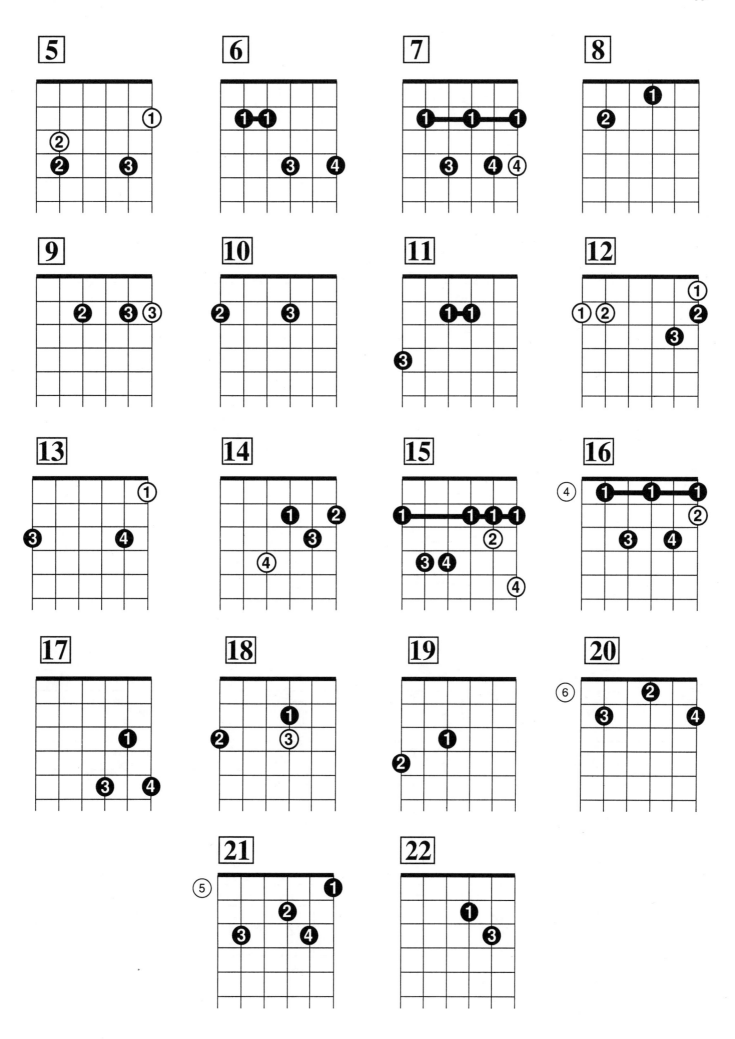

Pineapple Rag

Scott Joplin

SECTION IV

Open Tunings

Introduction

Open tunings are widely used in contemporary, fingerpicking guitar. Ry Cooder, Leo Kottke and John Fahey are some popular guitar players who frequently use open tunings.

An open tuning occurs when the open strings on the guitar are tuned to form a chord.

For example, the notes which make up the G Major chord are G, B and D. If we lower the first, fifth and sixth strings one tone, (2 frets), the notes of all the open strings now are D, G, D, G, B, D. We now have a G Major chord on the open strings, this is called open G tuning.

Open tunings give the guitar a different sound and tone depending on what tuning is used, because you can play chords you cannot normally position in standard tuning. The following pieces show four popular open tunings but there is an endless amount of different combinations the open strings can be tuned to. Only the tablature is shown because of the difficulty in reading open tuning guitar music.

Lesson 17
Open G Tuning

Open G tuning is the most popular open tuning and can be achieved by lowering the first string down a tone (2 frets) to D, the fifth string down a tone to G, and the sixth string down a tone to D also.

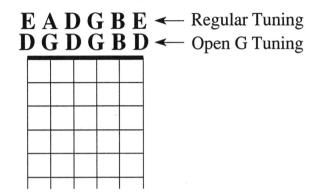

Once in open G tuning all the chords will have different shapes. Below are some of the popular chords used in open G tuning.

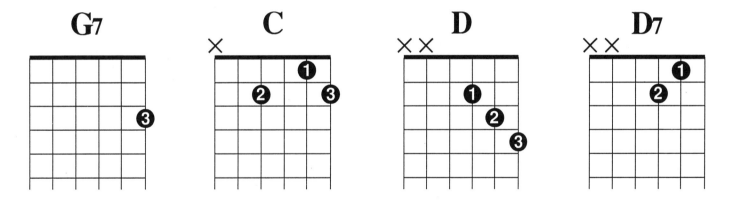

It is also useful to practise the open G tuning Blues scale.

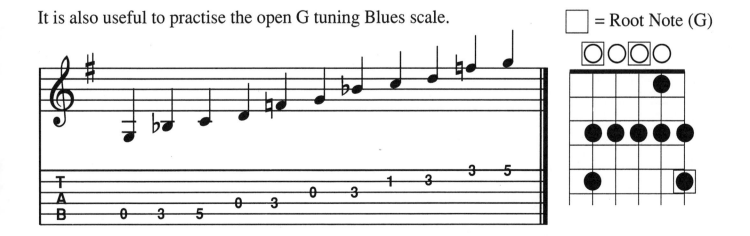

Jewels

Gee Wizz

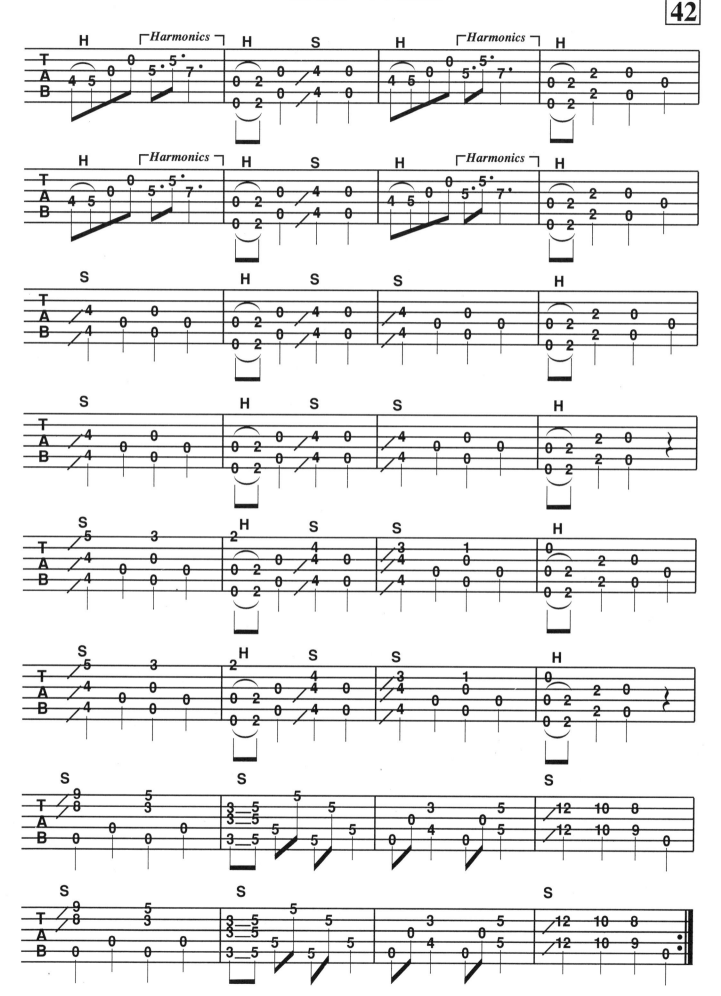

Lesson 18
Open D Tuning

Open D tuning is another popular tuning. To tune the guitar to this tuning the first, second and sixth string are lowered a tone (two frets) and the third string is lowered a semitone (one fret).

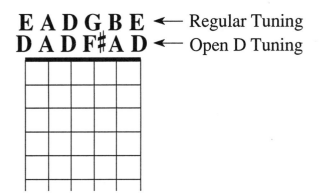

There are also some basic chords that are useful to know in open D tuning.

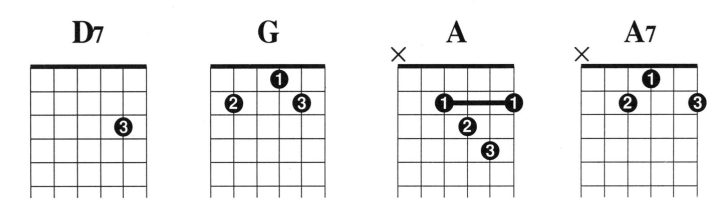

As with open G tuning it is also useful to understand the different fingering for the open D tuning Blues scale.

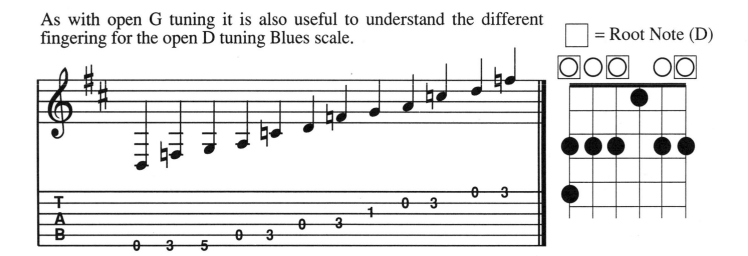

Siberia

Lesson 19
Open C Tuning

Open C tuning is not as widely used as the previous open tunings but has been included in this section because of its different sound. This tuning can be used to simulate the sound of a sitar. The second string is raised a semitone. The fourth and fifth strings are lowered a tone and the sixth string is lowered two tones from an "E" to a "C".

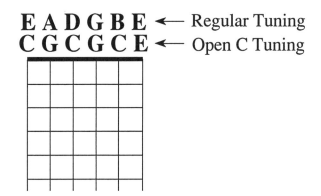

As with previous tunings some basic chords will be useful to know.

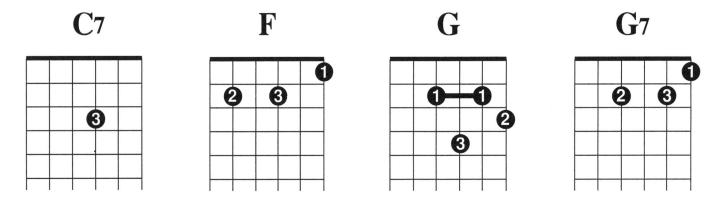

The C Blues scale can be played in almost three octaves in the first position.

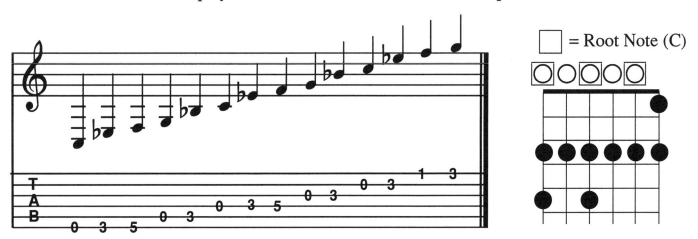

Backyard Boogie

𝄎 = an exact repeat of the previous two bars.

Lesson 20
Open E Tuning

Open E tuning is the same as open D tuning but is one tone higher in pitch. This causes a slightly different sound. To put the guitar in this tuning raise the third string a semitone and the fourth and fifth strings a tone.

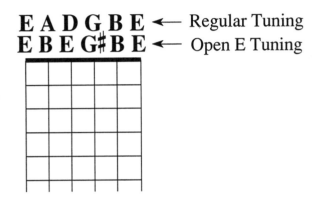

E A D G B E ← Regular Tuning
E B E G♯ B E ← Open E Tuning

The basic chord shapes are the same as the shapes in open D tuning, but the chords sound one tone higher.

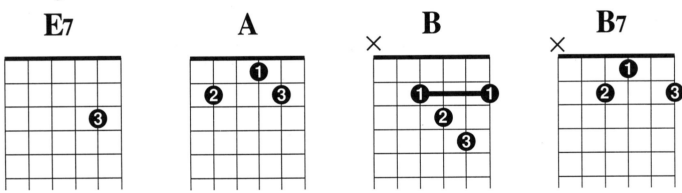

The fingering for the Blues scale is the same as the open D tuning Blues scale.

☐ = Root Note (E)

The Longest Mile

Country Stomp